0171

Masters of Music

ILLUSTRATED BY PAUL NEWLAND

DVOŘÁK

Masters of Music

DVOŘÁK

Percy M. Young

Ernest Benn Limited · London
David White · New York

FIRST PUBLISHED 1970

BY ERNEST BENN LIMITED

BOUVERIE HOUSE, FLEET STREET

LONDON, EC4

&

DAVID WHITE

60 EAST 55TH STREET, NEW YORK, NY10022

© PERCY M. YOUNG 1970

ILLUSTRATIONS © ERNEST BENN LIMITED 1970

PRINTED IN GREAT BRITAIN

ISBN 0 510–13717–2

LIBRARY OF CONGRESS CATALOG CARD NUMBER

U.S.A. 97250–241–4 *(Trade)*

87259–439–5 *(Library)*

Contents

Illustrations

Preface

A FRIEND READ THE MANUSCRIPT of this book and said: "Dvořák was a nice man!" That is a good summary; for in every way Dvořák was a nice man. More than that, he was a good man. And he was a great musician.

Dvořák is a persuasive composer. If one wished to convert someone to the idea that music is worth listening to one could do much worse than produce a recording of one of his works. Any work mentioned in this book would do. His music has a rare warmth of personality. This springs from two sources. Dvořák came from a part of Europe where there was a rich and living tradition of folk-song and folk-dance, the patterns of which he absorbed and communicated anew through his own inventions. He also had a great affection for people, believing that in the end their capacity for good would prevail over their tendency to evil. He shared many ideas with Josef Haydn, who also came from the eastern part of the one-time Austrian Empire, and there appear to be many similarities in musical outlook.

Haydn and Dvořák were simple men, of peasant origin. This enabled them to see many things clearly, and also to express themselves directly.

Dvořák belonged to a proud people with a long, often troubled, history. He knew this history and sought to express some part of it through his music. He aimed to speak for his own people—especially for those in his native village—to the people of the world. He believed in the importance of unimportant people. That he succeeded in his aim is a measure of his genuis. Dvořák is not only a Czech composer; he is for many of us today, in a special sense, Czechoslovakia.

Before Dvořák's day his countrymen who wished to make their mark in the world usually had to pretend to be something that they were not. Dvořák had no pretences. He was proud to be what he was. He was admired in many parts of Europe, in England, and in the United States. He made a particular contribution to the American tradition, as is described in Chapter 8.

Like all great men Dvořák was a visionary. He saw what should be done in the world and, symbolically at any rate, how it should be done. The secret of his philosophy is expressed in his own words on page 78.

I am grateful to the Librarian of the Royal College of Music, London, for drawing my attention to the communications from Dvořák to C. V. Stanford which are now in the possession of the Library.

P. M. Y.

1. *National Pride*

THE CZECH NATION has a history of a thousand years. Mostly it is a dark, tragic, history—a record of resistance to the aggression of powerful and ambitious neighbours. But it is relieved by acts of faith, and demonstrations of courage, that through the years have inspired many people in different parts of the world. The story of Czechoslovakia, or Bohemia as it was formerly called, is that of a Slavonic people who wished to preserve their own language, their own way of life, their own identity.

For those who live far away from the country the culture and thought of Czechoslovakia is likely often to be represented by Antonin Dvořák, the greatest of Czech musicians and the one who indisputably takes his place among the great masters of all time. More than most great masters Dvořák became the kind of composer he was because of the history of his people, and of this history his music is now a part.

A thousand years ago Bohemia became Christian and the names of two saints of that time are still held in veneration. The one was St Ludmilla, the other St Wenceslas. During the Middle Ages, when Charles IV was both Emperor of the Holy Roman Empire and King of Bohemia, Bohemia became a great centre of culture and learning. The Charles University, named after Charles IV, was founded and many of the fine Gothic buildings of the city erected at this time.

At the beginning of the fifteenth century a great patriot, John Huss, preached vehemently against corruption within the Catholic Church. He won great support, from rich and poor alike, not least of all because he preached in the language of the people. A religious reformer, Huss inspired his compatriots not only through speech but also through song, and a repertoire of chorales—derived in large part from an already strong folk-song tradition—was built up. In due course these chorales became popular in other countries, especially in Germany. John Huss suffered the fate of those who set conscience above expediency; he was called to account by the prospective Emperor and King of Bohemia, Sigismund, and Pope John XXII, and burned at the stake in 1415.

The Hussites fought for their cause for many years, and their valour was never forgotten. In 1883 Antonin Dvořák composed a *Hussite Overture*, which included two of the most famous of the hymns of the Hussites. The one is the chorale "Ye who are God's valiant warriors", the other the "Saint Wenceslas" chorale.

The Bohemians continued to struggle for religious freedom and for toleration for more than a hundred years. When the Thirty Years War—which had in the first place been caused by the Bohemian situation—came to an end, Bohemia was reduced to the status of a colony. Deserted by all the Protestants of Europe, the Bohemians had been defeated at the battle of the White Mountain on November 8, 1620. After that many of their leaders were executed, and many fled the country. Catholicism was made obligatory. The Czech language was discouraged and was soon only used by the peasantry. This phase of Czech history is recalled by Dvořák's *The Heirs of the White Mountain*, of 1872, a patriotic hymn which first brought him into prominence.

For many years those who wished to advance themselves

The Týn Church and John Huss Monument, Prague

felt obliged virtually to renounce Czech nationality. It was, as many musicians discovered, prudent to follow the general fashion of western Europe. Christoph Willibald Gluck (1714–87) was born and brought up near Prague; but as soon as possible he made his way to Vienna, from where, with Austrian credentials, he could more easily make his way in the opera houses of Europe.

The first public theatre was opened in Prague in 1737. In the first place this existed for the performance of Italian operas and ballets, and German plays, for an aristocracy that on the whole preferred to preserve privilege than the Czech tradition. From time to time, however, plays in Czech were given. In 1781 Joseph II, who wished to liberalise his Empire in order to prevent its disruption, abolished serfdom and introduced various measures of toleration. This gave some encouragement to the Bohemians, and in 1786 a new "Imperial and Royal Patriotic Czech Theatre" was established. Until a theatre intended for drama of a national character was built in 1862 most of the productions of this organisation took place in the Estates Theatre (now known as the Tyl Theatre).

The attitude of Joseph II and the ideals of liberty let loose by the French Revolution led to a considerable relaxation of hard-line discipline within the Austrian dominions. The desire for national liberation or, at least, for the possibility of a free expression of national identity intensified during the years of the Napoleonic Wars. When these came to an end, Bohemia—like every other small nation at that time— waited for the great powers to understand and support its claims. Alas, small nations, each conscious only of its own particular heritage and interests, were easy prey for the large powers. But the impulses renewed during the first part of the nineteenth century were strong, and were to determine the quality and fervour of Dvořák's music.

From the beginning of the nineteenth century interest in Czech history and culture was stimulated by the scholar František Palacký who wrote the first *History of the Czech Nation*. A group of young intellectuals sought to extend this interest. Among them was a lawyer, František Jan Škroup (1801-62), who was also a musician. Škroup helped to arrange operas sung in Czech for the Estates Theatre, and in 1826 he composed the music for *The Tinker*, written by J. K. Chmelenský. *The Tinker* was a great success, and provided an incentive for Czech composers to create their own operatic tradition. But, as Dvořák somewhat bitterly pointed out to an English friend when he was in London, until 1862 Czech opera singers were only permitted to sing in their own language in their own country on occasional Sundays. Škroup's opera is important historically but the music is no longer known. One work of this composer, however, is known and loved by Czechs the world over. This is *Kde domuv můj?* (*Where is my Home?*) which became the national anthem of Czechoslovakia.

The words of this hymn were written by Josef Kajetán Tyl (1808-53) a writer whose own life was an inspiration to his compatriots. After the Revolution of 1848 Tyl was so persecuted by the Imperial authorities, who alleged that he was a subversive influence, that he was unable to find regular work. He wandered from place to place, as a travelling player. In 1882 a play on Tyl's life was performed at the so-called "Temporary" Theatre, Prague. The overture was composed by Dvořák, who made Škroup's melody for *Where is My Home?* one of its two principal motivs, or themes. Throughout the overture the listener is aware of the general shape of this melody, which is shown in different forms. In the coda (end section), however, it is given directly and proudly in a full blaze of orchestral tone.

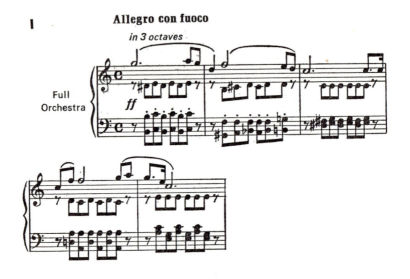

2. *Learning the Hard Way*

ANTONIN DVOŘÁK was born on September 8, 1841, in the village of Nelahozeves (then known by the German name Mühlhausen), some 40 miles north of Prague on the river Vltava. His father was the village innkeeper and butcher; his mother had been a servant in the household of the Lobkowitz family. The village was dominated by their castle, which is a famous example of Czech Renaissance architecture. On the opposite bank of the river there was another castle, a splendid Baroque building known as the Castle of Veltrusy. In later years his memories of this village and its inhabitants inspired Dvořák to compose his opera *The Jacobin*. There is also a smaller piece by which the village is remembered, the third of the set of *Poetic Pictures* (Op. 85), of 1889. This is called "On the Old Castle".

2

Dr Charles Burney—the English musical historian— passed by that way in the 1770s and while he disliked the "sour milk and black sour bread" that was all he could find

Antonín Dvořák

to eat he was greatly impressed with the musical ability of
the children. Even then they had compulsory music in
school, and it did not dampen their enthusiasm for music
out of school. They were taught music by the village schoolmaster, who was also the church organist, and what they
learned from him was supplemented by the travelling musicians who came at fair time. In Burney's day musical education was encouraged by the nobility so that in due course
they would have an adequate supply of servants qualified to
provide reasonable entertainment for guests.

One of those home-bred musicians was Jan Hugo Václav
Vořišek (1791–1825), whose father had been a village
schoolmaster. Having learned music from his father Vořišek
was employed by the Lobkowitz family living in Dvořák's

village. With their support he was able to make his way to Vienna, where he met Beethoven, who himself was befriended by Prince Lobkowitz, and finally gained a court appointment. A fine composer Voříšek drew on the resources of native Bohemian music in respect both of melody and rhythm. His *Impromptus* were popular in Vienna and it was partly because he knew them that Franz Schubert composed his *Impromptus*.

The Bohemian landscape was very beautiful. When Dvořák was a child the way of life was as it had been for centuries. The nobility, who were more often away from their country houses than they were in residence, enjoyed prosperity and relative idleness. The rest of the population worked hard and usually did what they were told.

The Dvořáks were poor and had eight children to bring up. Antonin went to the village school and learned the rudiments of music, including violin-playing from Josef Spitz, a well-loved teacher. At the age of twelve, however, he was sent to school in Zlonice, a small town to the east of Nelahozeves. Antonin, who had already helped out in the butcher's shop, went to Zlonice in order to improve his prospects in that trade by learning German. He was fortunate that his mother's brother was willing both to house him and to pay for his education, and that the schoolmaster, Antonin Liehmann, was a many-sided man. He was a capable German instructor, a reasonably good organist, and the director of a local orchestra. Liehmann is immortalised in the character of Benda, in *The Jacobin* (see p. 56), to describe whom Dvořák reserved some of his most affectionate music.

The Dvořák family moved house from Nelahozeves to Zlonice because the father felt that he could do better trade in the larger place—even though it meant leaving many old friends. Antonin, somewhat in disgrace on account of his indifferent success in learning German, was sent away to another school; this time to Česka Kamenice on the German frontier, where it was hoped he would make more progress. From the point of view of the elder Dvořák this experiment, unfortunately, was anything but satisfactory. All that happened was that the boy became more and more involved in music. This was all very well, but it would not combine professionally very well with butchery. In this craft Antonin did show some ability, and if he were to persevere the reasoning was that he would achieve a greater prosperity than through music.

Antonin did what was expected of him. He returned to Zlonice and conscientiously set about turning himself into a tradesman. He even got a certificate of competence in the slaughter of sheep. But he went on doggedly having lessons with Liehmann, and Liehmann began to think highly of his ability. In due course the teacher sided with rebellion. Antonin did not want to be a butcher; he did want to be a musician. But to become an adequate musician in a competitive world a thorough training was necessary. This was available so far as a boy in Dvořák's position was concerned only in Prague.

In the autumn of 1857 Antonin, having been admitted to the School of Organists in the city, arrived in Prague as a student. Fortunately for him his uncle, who had no children of his own, was able and willing to make a modest contribution towards his living expenses. The head of the School at the time of Dvořák's arrival was Karel Pitsch (1786–1858): After his death—during Dvořák's second student year—Josef Krejči (1821–81) took his place. Krejči was a well-known composer of church music, who had fixed views about

The family house and birthplace of Dvořák at Nelahozeves

music in general. He considered Dvořák a satisfactory student of practical music, but he complained that he was below standard in theory. He also drew attention to his continuing incompetence in the German language.

So far as his later reputation was concerned Krejči was unfortunate that he had the temerity to write a true report (as it seemed to him) on a promising pupil who could do better. But the promising pupil turned out to be a genius. In that Krejči advised a proper knowledge of German his advice was sound. But he does not deserve abuse for any apparent lack of patriotism, for in the revolutionary year of 1848 he had founded the first musical journal to be published in the Czech language.

Although after his graduation he was qualified to practice as a church organist Dvořák had no intention immediately of doing so. Instead he decided to stay on in Prague, and to support himself he joined Karel Komzák's orchestra—a group of players well-known in the cafés of the city. Dvořák's pay was slender in the extreme. He looked towards an uncertain future, but not without hope.

In 1848 the Austrian Empire was shaken by revolts in Vienna itself, in Prague, in Milan, in Budapest, and in Illyria. Although independently inspired (had there been any effective unity of aim the Empire would have collapsed) all these revolts had as the main objective the liberation of national traditions, and then a consequent decentralisation of government was hoped for. Austrian administration was severely stretched during the next decade and when the French and the Sardinians declared war on the Austrians in 1859 with a view to freeing Lombardy and Venetia, catastrophe could only be prevented by some loosening of the rein in other subject territories. In 1866 the Austrian armies were defeated by those of Prussia at Sadowa in eastern Bohemia. It was in this period of seven years that Czech nationalism reached a climax, and Dvořák found the direction he should follow.

One of those about whose political views there was no doubt in 1848 was the composer Bedřich Smetana (1824–84). Fired by revolutionary zeal he had composed a march for the Students' Legion, and a nationalistic *Solemn Overture*. The years that followed were difficult for him and, like many Czechs before and since, he went abroad in 1856, taking an appointment as conductor of a musical society in Gothenburg in Sweden. In 1861 Smetana returned home, to find a new enthusiasm in the air, a new sense of purpose

Bedřich Smetana

among the intellectuals who were the true leaders of national
revival. These included Karel Erben, a pioneer in collecting
folk-song (see p. 70); Božena Nemcová, the first Czech
woman novelist; Jan Neruda (1834–91), a master of
characterisation in fiction; Vitežslav Hálek (1835–74), a
nature poet; as well as a number of artists. Of these the
leader was Josef Mánes (1820–71), who was bringing a new
vigour into painting and illustration by his studies of Czech
life and custom. Between 1856 and 1862 he made many
drawings based on subjects from folk-song, thus providing
a link between the visual and aural arts. To bring a Czech
National Theatre into being, however, was still uphill work;
but on November 18, 1862, out of the funds that had been

collected for this purpose, the so-called "Temporary" Theatre was opened. It was here that all Czech plays and operas were performed until the opening of the National Theatre on June 11, 1881.

When the "Temporary" Theatre was started the orchestra was recruited from Komzák's players. Dvořák, therefore, found himself playing the viola in opera performances two or three times a week. To add to his earnings, he also joined a group which gave performances in a lunatic asylum. In this he anticipated Edward Elgar, who, for the same reason, had similar experience as a young man.

3. *A National Opera*

THE FIRST CZECH OPERA to be performed at the "Temporary" Theatre was *Vladimir, God's Chosen* by František Skuherský (1830–92). This production took place on September 27, 1863. Two years later, on January 5, 1866, Smetana's opera *The Brandenburgers in Bohemia* was performed, the composer conducting. On May 30, 1866, Smetana's most famous opera—and one of the best-loved of all operas—was given its premiere. This was *The Bartered Bride*, a gay, romantic picture of Bohemian village life.

Dvořák played in the orchestra at these and other performances, and all the time wondered when his turn would come. Very few people even knew that Dvořák composed, and of those that did some were more amused than impressed. Dvořák was from the provinces, and he was somewhat shy and diffident; but he was also obstinate and industrious. Being as he was, and living when he did, he had a number of conflicts to resolve. The first came from a recognition of class distinction; the second from the extension of this into the national field.

When he was a student Dvořák lived with an aunt, but having graduated he preferred the greater freedom (if less comfort) of an apartment kept by a fellow member of Komzák's orchestra. He had very little money on which to live, and was only able to have access to scores and to a piano through the kindness of Karel Bendl (1838–97) who was himself a musician of promise, and the first really to appreciate Dvořák's talents. Like Dvořák, Bendl was the son of an innkeeper—but one who had prospered.

In order to eke out his living Dvořák gave piano lessons. Among his pupils were Josefina and Anna Cermáková, daughters of a prosperous goldsmith. He fell in love with Josefina, a member of the Czech Theatre, but she promptly walked off and married Count Václav Kaunic. In accordance with romantic convention Dvořák got rid of his disappointment by writing music; in this case a set of songs entitled *Cypresses*. When Josefina removed herself from consideration as a girl-friend, however, Dvořák appreciated the qualities in her sister that he had not previously noticed. He courted Anna for seven years and in 1872 they were married.

The seven years that lay between falling in love with Josefina and marriage with Anna were pretty heart-breaking. A young composer at that time was pulled in two, if not three, directions. Classical standards—exemplified in the sonata style—laid one set of obligations on him; Romanticism, with all its hints of freedom, another. The young composer aiming at the international market had Beethoven on one side, Wagner and Liszt on the other. Behind the intention to become a composer, so far as Dvořák was concerned, was the further duty of becoming a Czech composer.

In 1865 Dvořák entered a work—a symphony—for a competition in Germany. He was unsuccessful and the score was never returned. Twenty years after the composer's death the manuscript was recovered, and the first performance of Dvořák's First Symphony took place in Brno in 1936. This symphony was said by Dvořák himself at first to have had the subtitle "Bells of Zlonice". In general it may be said to be autobiographical, incorporating the hopes and

Dvořák and his wife, Anna

fears of his early days in Zlonice. It follows the structural
methods of Beethoven fairly closely but shows the influence
of later thought in the evocative use of motiv. Motivs —
brief themes, or parts of themes (see p. 15) — were much
used in the later part of the nineteenth century after the

manner of Berlioz, Liszt, and Wagner. A motiv, intended first usually to define a character, a mood, or a place, was threaded through a composition. Thus it was termed a *Leitmotiv* ("lead-motiv"), and was shown in different forms. In Examples 6a and 6b (p. 43–4), for instance, two variants on one motiv may be seen. In both cases the tune looks the same, but there are subtle differences in the sound. In Dvořák's First Symphony an important motiv understandably sounds like bells.

3

In the autumn of 1865 Dvořák completed a Second Symphony. This work also had to wait a long time until it could be played, the first performance (of a revised version) taking place in 1888. If the First Symphony expressed the disappointments as well as the determination of youth, the Second recollects rather its pleasures, and the ability of youth to appreciate beauty. This Symphony in B flat is, so to speak, a "Spring Symphony". In its lyrical character it shows how much Dvořák was influenced by Schubert (who, in turn, had been influenced by Voříšek and other Czech musicians living in Vienna). But it also shows a strong characteristic of all the outstanding Bohemian and Magyar composers, by introducing a distinctive musical imagery for giving expression to and depicting nature. In the second movement of his Second Symphony the sounds of birds and of the rustling trees of the Bohemian woodlands are to be heard.

Throughout Dvořák's music there is this powerful sense of communion with nature. That nature was becoming part of a Bohemian musician's vision is suggested by Václav Tomašek (1774–1850), who related in his *Autobiography* (1845) how he had introduced melodies and harmonies in his *Eclogues* that belonged to the shepherd musicians of his country. As we shall see, Dvořák, too, transferred sounds direct from the music of the countryside.

As well as composing two symphonies Dvořák at this time also wrote a cello concerto and some chamber music. In due course he disposed of many of his early works, but not before trying some of them out at private gatherings. A few people began to notice that he was a composer, but not many gave much hope for his future. Under the general influence of Smetana, and believing that a good Czech composer should show himself as a good Czech, Dvořák wrote an opera in 1870. This was *Alfred the Great*, based on a poem by Franz Schubert's friend Karl Theodor Körner (1791–1813). In a society whose censorship was strict the only way to make a point was to do so by allusion. King Alfred's fight against the Danes was symbolic of that of the Czechs against the Austrians for those who wished to take it that way. Under the influence of Wagner Dvořák wrote an opera that wanted nothing in the way of *Leitmotiv* or complex instrumentation. It was not, however, stageworthy, and only the overture survived. This was played and published only after Dvořák's death. First called the "Tragic" it is now described as the "Dramatic" Overture.

In 1872 Dvořák's next venture in the field of opera met with partial success. The overture to *The King and the Charcoal Burner* was played at one of Smetana's concerts. Both singers and instrumentalists, however, complained that the music was too complicated to be worthwhile rehearsing. In an attempt to oblige them Dvořák rewrote the work, but

without being able to persuade the directors of the theatre
that the revised version could hold its place in the repertory.
In 1874 he made another attempt at setting a Czech subject,
turning *The Stubborn Lovers*, by Josef Štolba, into a one-act
opera. It was not to be performed, however, until 1881.

But Dvořák now had at last broken through to gain some
degree of wider recognition. On March 9, 1873, his *Hymnus*
(a setting of Hálek's *The Heirs of the White Mountain*) was
performed by the Hlahol Choral Society of which Smetana
had been, and Bendl at the time was, conductor. Critics who
previously had spoken censoriously of Dvořák's music as
being too "Wagnerian", or too "formless', or too "modern",
recognised that in this work Dvořák was saying something
that they wanted to be said. Music conveying an ideal that
was held in common suddenly appeared as more important
than music which was just music.

The patriotism that inspired the *Hymnus* also inspired the
Third Symphony in E flat, which Dvořák completed during
the June of 1873 and which Smetana conducted at a concert
on March 30, 1874. This symphony, showing Wagnerian
influence in the rich string and harp scoring of the middle
movement, extends the heroic sentiment of the *Hymnus* into
symphonic expression. The work is in three movements,
bound together by the forceful motiv (built on the interval
of the fourth) that occurs in the "Bells of Zlonice" Symphony.
This symphony expresses love of country, sadness at its
troubles, hope in its future—the main themes, perhaps, of
all Dvořák's music.

With the example of Liszt before him Dvořák intended
at this time to compose a series of *Slavonic Rhapsodies*. In
the autumn of 1874 the first of such pieces was composed,
but, being in the end the only one of its kind, was described

merely as *Rhapsody in A minor*. Firm, fervent, energetic, and finally triumphant, this again leaves no doubt as to its composer's patriotic intention.

In the meanwhile Dvořák was earning his living as organist of St Adalbert's Church, this occupation being both more respectable and slightly more remunerative than that of viola player. St Adalbert's—a Gothic building of the period of Charles IV but altered into Baroque in the eighteenth century—was almost on the river bank. It was convenient to the "Slavonic Island" (Slovanský Ostrov), which was then a centre of cultural life, and where Liszt, Berlioz, and Wagner at various times had all given concerts.

4. *An Award from the Government*

IN 1869 JOHANNES BRAHMS (1833–97) settled in Vienna. Three years later he was elected to one of the most important musical positions in the city, the Directorship of the Society of Friends of Music. Among his other appointments was membership of a Government Commission responsible for the disposal of bursaries for promising and poor artists in the Empire. The critic Eduard Hanslick (1825–1904) was a fellow member.

As organist of St Adalbert's Church Dvořák earned 120 gulden a year, to which he was able to add another 60 gulden from private teaching (altogether then about £15 in English money). He did not see why he should not apply for a government grant. But first he must suffer the indignity of writing to the Town Clerk of Prague, on June 15, 1874, in this manner:

> Dear Sir: I should be obliged if you would be good enough to furnish me with a certificate in German confirming that I am without means, as such a certificate must be enclosed with my application for the award of a State grant for artists. . . .

The certificate having been duly supplied Dvořák submitted his Symphony in E flat, and other works, to the panel of judges in Vienna. Brahms liked what he saw, and so did

Johannes Brahms

Hanslick. Dvořák, therefore, was awarded a grant worth 400 gulden at the time when it was needed; not so much to enable him to live as to boost his self-confidence.

It says much for Brahms's objectivity that he, the acknowledged leader of the anti-Wagner school, could so heartily commend Dvořák's music, in which there were strong traces of Wagner. It is also remarkable that Hanslick, who was born in Prague but was not interested in Czech culture as such, could also support his claims.

Dvořák was fortunate enough to be given a State award each year for four years running, and that this was so was largely due to Brahms's sponsorship. In 1877 Brahms wrote to his own publisher, Fritz Simrock, in Berlin, recommending him particularly to publish a set of *Airs from Moravia*, for 2 voices and piano, which Dvořák had submitted for consideration that year. Although the texts were Czech Brahms saw no reason why they could not be translated into German. Indeed, he wondered whether some had not already been translated by Joseph Wenzig (1807–76), of Prague, one of Smetana's librettists, who was well-known to him as a translator. It is interesting at this point to notice that Brahms himself had come under Bohemian influence. In the first set of his 9 *Songs* (Op. 69) he had set three of Wenzig's translations from Czech, and one from Slovak, and he had not neglected to work into his music certain details from Czech folk-music idiom.

On the strength of his bursaries Dvořák gave up playing the organ at church, and also moved house. His creative energy was amazing. Between 1875 and 1878 he composed songs, a considerable number of chamber works, the Symphony in F major, part of that in D minor, a Piano Concerto, *Symphonic Variations on an original Theme* (Op. 78), and the operas *Wanda* and *The Cunning Peasant*. *Wanda*, based on a Polish legend, was given a successful first performance, but it did not stay in the repertoire. *The Cunning Peasant*, of which the libretto was modelled somewhat after the model of *The Bartered Bride*, was more durable. It was performed in Dresden and Hamburg, as well as in Prague, but was forbidden in Vienna on political grounds.

The *Symphonic Variations* were performed at the "Temporary" Theatre, Prague, on December 2, 1877, but then

Scene from a performance of The Cunning Peasant *at the Smetana Theatre in Prague*

had to wait until taken up with some enthusiasm by Hans Richter and established in the repertoire by him. The *Stabat Mater* was written out of private grief. Within a short space of time three of Dvořák's children had died; but it was not until 1880 that the work written in their memory was first heard. Dvořák's way to the top was anything but easy.

At first he was handicapped because of his nationality. In the German-dominated market the Czechs were at a disadvantage. However, at this time Dvořák was responding to the call for national music made by Dr Ludevit Procházka (a famous conductor) by setting more Czech poems to music. He chose a number by the great poet Hálek—who had died in 1874—and they were collectively known as *Evening Songs*. Some of these settings by Dvořák were published in Op. 3, some in Op. 9, and some in Op. 31. In the third song of Op. 3, *I am that knight of fairy tale*, the story of the Czech nation, perhaps, is symbolised. "I am the knight who proudly went forth to the world to see a fair maid. But, it was said, whoever should see her would be cursed. I thought that that could not mean me. I sought and saw the maid—and suffered the curse. So, now I must be a minstrel." Dvořák sets the words with simplicity—with note groups repeated as in folk-music—but with a fierce energy:

Once the publisher Simrock realised that Brahms had not recommended merely a lame duck to him he considered how best he could capitalise on Dvořák's genius. The *Moravian Duets* had sold well enough. Brahms's *Hungarian Dances* had been sensationally successful. National idioms (whether presented authentically or not) had become saleable ever since the smaller nations of Europe had started pressing their claims in the political arena. So Simrock commissioned a set of *Slavonic Dances* from Dvořák. These dances (Op. 46), written first for piano duet and later orchestrated, were at once successful—beyond the publisher's expectations and the composer's wildest dreams. The *Slavonic Dances* (a second set appeared in 1886) were not arrangements of actual peasant dances—but a commentary on and evocation of their spirit. Dvořák knew and loved folk-song and folk-dance in every detail, but he did not intend to become their slave. When the first set of *Slavonic Dances* were being composed he had other similar enterprises in mind, notably the three *Slavonic Rhapsodies* (Op. 45) and the *Czech Suite* (op. 39). The first two of the *Rhapsodies* were included in a programme of Dvořák's works which the composer himself conducted at the "Temporary" Theatre on November 17, 1878.

That was altogether an encouraging year. Dvořák had been writing chamber music for years. Now it was welcomed by the greatest chamber music player in the world at that time—Joseph Joachim (1831–1907), the violinist. Joachim gratefully took up the Sextet in A for 2 violins, 2 violas, 2 cellos (Op. 48), composed in 1878, and the Quartet in E flat (Op. 51). At the end of the year Dvořák travelled to Vienna so that he could personally give to him the score of the Quartet in D minor (Op. 34) which was dedicated to

Brahms. It was shortly before his excursion to Vienna that Dvořák expressed his feelings to Brahms in a letter—"I can", he wrote, "only say that I shall all my life owe you the deepest gratitude for your good and noble intentions towards me, which are worthy of a truly great artist and man."

Brahms had benefited from the friendship and generous encouragement of Robert Schumann. Dvořák benefited from the kindness of Brahms. On his way back from Vienna he stopped off at Brno, where he was greeted by a young man whom he in his turn had befriended. This was Leoš Janáček (1854–1928) who had come to know Dvořák when studying at the Prague Organ School in 1874. Now, four years later, Janáček was back in Brno, where he had attended college, as conductor of the local choral society. In 1885 Janáček acknowledged his debt to Dvořák both in the dedication and the style of his *Four male voice choruses* of that year.

5. *A National Composer*

DVOŘÁK BECAME recognised as a national figure somewhere about 1880, when it was clear that the distinctively Czech music that he composed was making its mark in the wider world. People could point to, say, the *Slavonic Dances*, and be reminded that the Czechs as a people did exist, that there was a particular Czech cultural heritage. Some could even come to question a political situation which made the Czechs a subject people.

Dvořák was by no means the only composer who fulfilled this function of being a national mouthpiece. Stanislaw Moniuszko (1819–72) expressed Polish nationalism; Ferencz Erkel (1810–93) was the father of Hungarian nationalism in music; Edvard Grieg (1843–1907), making full use of his country's musical traditions, first gave Norway a place on the musical map.

The problem common to all these composers was how to escape from the overpowering influence of German music. In every case the distinctive rhythms of national dance were a help. A still greater help was language. Dvořák was well aware of the importance of language and he was reluctant to use any other but his own, even when it would have been advantageous to do so. His resistance to learning German as a boy was soundly based—he knew that the Czech language, despised by those who aspired to social eminence, was strong and beautiful; that its patterns and rhythms in some way enshrined the faith of the nation.

The Czech language differs from most others because it

lacks the preliminary weak beat that causes the rhythmic feature, particularly common in English, known as *anacrusis*. It will be noticed that many of Dvořák's themes begin on a strong beat and in this they show a marked difference from those of Smetana. That this is the case is due to the differences in the upbringing of the two composers.

Smetana, the son of the brewer to Count Waldstein (another patron of Beethoven), was brought up in more or less comfortable circumstances. From his boyhood he was accustomed to speak German, and it was only in later life that he felt that he ought to learn Czech. Dvořák, on the other hand, was brought up in a Czech-speaking community. Czech was his mother tongue, and he was proud of it. His reluctance to learn German was a sign of protest, not only on behalf of the Czech people in general, but of those of his native village in particular. Dvořák had a great loyalty to those among whom he was brought up, and an instinctive loyalty to their institutions and customs. His nationalism was as deep and as simple as that. So that when it came to the matter of folk-music he had no other thought than that this was a part of the way of life, and, as this was so, then he was bound to reflect it in his own music. Dvořák could have said—as Elgar once did in respect of his music—"I am folk-music".

Characteristics of folk-song melody are to be found in Dvořák's original melodies. The theme of the *Symphonic Variations* shows some of these characteristics. In this instance it is not, perhaps, altogether surprising, since this was originally a tune to accompany words. Notice also the simple, but effective, way in which the theme is accompanied.

5

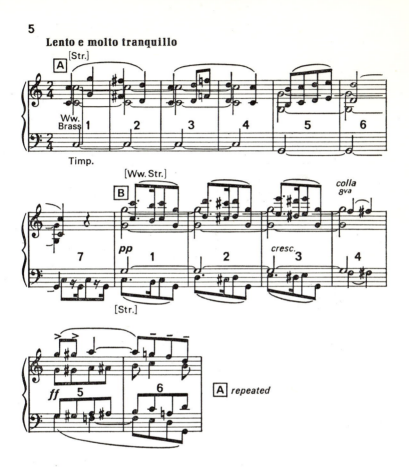

Here there are to be noticed a strong beat start, and an irregularity in the balance of phrases. (A) is 7 bars long; (B) is 6 bars long. The tune commences with a rising fifth, and then a series of descending notes occur. The third note F sharp, is outside the tonality of C major, but will be found in one of the older scales, or modes. This feature is also to be

View of the Charles Bridge, Prague

found in the "Bridal dance" tune in *The Wild Dove* (see Ex. 6b p. 44).

The music examples given in this book show how often Dvořák used the melodic interval of the fourth (see the accompaniment, bars 4–5, above). In one very attractive work, the *Serenade* for 10 wind instruments (Op. 44), all four movements have opening melodies that begin with this figure.

While similarities between Dvořák's melodic shapes and that of folk-song are evident, those between his rhythms and those of folk-dance are even more marked. The elements of folk-music were the vernacular of musical speech, and Dvořák picked up the vernacular and used it for his own purposes. It is often difficult to know where folk-music ends and Dvořák begins, especially in respect of rhythm. His rhythms are distinctive, and full of life, and owed much to such dances as the *skočná* and the *polka* (2-time dances), to the *furiant* (3-time with cross-accents), the *dumka* (a lament, with slow and quick contrasting sections), and variants of mazurka, minuet, and waltz. These dances, and many others, were not only Czech, but belonged to the Slavonic tradition in general.

Dvořák absorbed not only the melodic and rhythmic features of folk-music but also its distinctive colour. It is this colour which gives a special quality to his orchestration. There is a particular richness here, especially in the manner in which woodwind instruments are used. The "Bridal Scene" from *The Wild Dove* in brief space shows how original Dvořák was in his handling of folk idiom.

6a

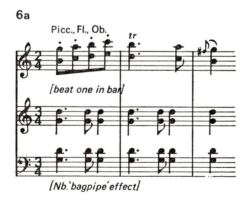

6b

[Waltz]   x compare Ex. 5

Nationalism is sometimes regarded as a province of Romanticism. Composers who cared to be described as "nationalists", living in the Romantic period, naturally made use of many of the techniques of Romanticism. Dvořák's harmonic methods, by which he obtained the greatest possible emotional satisfaction from chords and chordal contrasts, were a continuation of those of Schubert and Schumann.

Dvořák was a highly professional composer. He had emerged from the lower ranks of professional music as few others of the Romantic era had done. His knowledge of music was from the inside, from the viola player's desk. He knew instinctively what would work and what would not. This is why his orchestral works and chamber music are so practicable.

When he was nearing forty years of age Dvořák was recognised as an "original "composer. His originality is not quite obvious, for it consists of a combination of various aspects of music, none of which are entirely unfamiliar. What this combination signified was the point of view of a Czech composer. This is, perhaps, the more meaningful because it is so directly expressed. Dvořák knew the virtues of simplicity. He learned them at Nelahozeves.

Now, in the late 1870s, to some extent able to please himself, Dvořák tried to leave Prague for the country during the summer. He was a countryman and loved every aspect of country life, from which he sought inspiration for composition. In the summer of 1879 he stayed at Sychrov. In the following summer he was the guest of his brother-in-law, at Vysoká, near Príbram, in the hills 50 miles southwest of Prague. During these years he composed the Violin Concerto in A minor (Op. 53) which had been commissioned by Joachim and which considerably revised to satisfy Joachim's criticism; the Symphony in D major (Op. 60), dedicated to Hans Richter; the opera *Dimitri;* the incidental music for *Josef Kajetán Tyl* (see p. 15); the Quartet in C major (Op. 61); and a number of smaller works which included the *Seven Gypsy Songs* (Op. 55), to which Dvořák's most popular song, "Songs my mother taught me", belonged. The most beautiful song in this collection, however, is "Silent Woods", which mirrors the countryside which Dvořák loved. The effect of the dropping thirds in the melody is quite magical:

7

Moderato

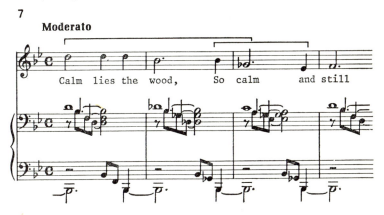

Calm lies the wood, So calm and still

followed by (melody)

Such small works were welcomed by his publisher, who found them immensely profitable, and Dvořák wrote them with considerable pleasure. He did not disregard the interests of less sophisticated music-lovers; nor did he find it at all improper to earn his living by satisfying these interests.

Hans Richter (1843–1916), conductor of the Vienna Philharmonic Orchestra, began to conduct orchestras in England in 1877. He remained an effective influence in British musical life for more than thirty years. When Richter praised a composer the British took notice. He praised Dvořák, and before long Dvořák was invited to visit England. This proved to be a turning-point in his career.

6. *Dvořák in England*

DVOŘÁK'S MUSIC, as has been suggested, was not entirely unknown in England. Some of the *Slavonic Dances* had been performed by the Crystal Palace Orchestra, conducted by August Manns, in 1879. The programme note on this occasion stated that

> so little is [Dvořák's name] known, even in Germany, that it has been found impossible to obtain any information as to his position and antecedents, or the nature of his works, which, it will be observed, have reached their 46th opus.

The comment "even in Germany" is an indication of the standing of the Czech people at that time in other countries. However, Joseph Bennett, the critic and librettist, and a friend of Arthur Sullivan, did his best to correct faulty impressions by publishing a long article on Dvořák in the April and May issues of *The Musical Times* in 1881.

After close consideration of Dvořák's music Bennett concluded:

> . . . The result of his work must be to strenghten the movement which is now so eagerly drawing thematic material from folk-music, and to enrich the common musical language of all countries with new, diversified, and precious resources.

This was a generous prelude to Dvořák's first visit to England. The publishing house of Novello, meanwhile, was trying to have the vocal score of the *Stabat Mater* ready in time for the Birmingham Festival of 1882, but this they were unable to do, having been held up by the dilatoriness of Simrock, in Berlin. They were able to publish it during the next year, however, and the first performance of the *Stabat Mater* in England was given by the London Musical Society, conducted by Joseph Barnby, in April, 1883.

Before he came to England Dvořák was conscious that efforts were being made there on his behalf, and on September 10, 1883, he wrote to Manns thanking him for his interest and drawing his attention to the Violin Concerto, the *Nocturne* for Strings (Op. 40), and the *Scherzo Capriccioso* (Op. 66). The last of these is a powerful, turbulent work, relieved by a tranquil melody given at first to the cor anglais (or "English horn"), an instrument for which Dvořák had a particular liking.

In March, 1884, Dvořák conducted the Symphony in D major and the *Hussite Overture* for the Philharmonic Society, the *Stabat Mater* at a concert at the Albert Hall, and the *Nocturne* and *Scherzo Capriccioso*, which he had previously recommended to Manns, at the Crystal Palace. On March 21 he wrote this touching note to his father:

> In some of the [English] papers there was also mention made of you, that I come of poor parents and that my father was a butcher and innkeeper in Nelahozeves and did everything to give his son a proper education. *Honour be to you for that.*

In the summer Dvořák was elected an Honorary Member of the Philharmonic Society, which news he responded to with a letter, in English, to the Society:

I have received your letter and thank you for it. The news of the rarely distinction give me very great honour and pleasure.

I take my liberty to pay you mine greatest thankfulness to express to the directory of the celebrated Philharmonic Society.

In the autumn Dvořák returned to England to conduct the *Stabat Mater* and the D major Symphony at the Three Choirs Festival in Worcester. Edward Elgar (1857–1934) played the violin in the orchestra, and wrote to a friend:

I wish you could hear Dvořák's music. It is simply ravishing, so tuneful and clever and the orchestration is wonderful: no matter how few instruments he uses it never sounds thin. I cannot describe it; it must be heard.

On March 24, 1885, Dvořák conducted his Symphony in D minor for the Philharmonic Society. This great symphony is filled with a great sense of passion; it is a record of struggle and a statement of faith. It is also highly personal. At the time Dvořák was finding recognition in the world as a composer among composers. Hanslick wished him to leave Prague and to live in Vienna, where he could write "German" operas. The Berlin publisher refused Dvořák's request that the titles of his works as well as his name should be printed in Czech as well as in German. It is not surprising then the D minor Symphony should show evidence of struggle and a determination to surmount difficulties, nor that some of the melodies should bear resemblances to melodies in the *Hussite Overture*. As evidence of Dvořák's feeling on the subject of nationality it is worth noticing that when he was in London in 1885 the Club of German Artists

D

invited him to dine with them. He refused, saying that he was not a German artist.

Meanwhile Dvořák had composed the cantata *The Spectre's Bride* for the Birmingham Festival. This was given its first performance on August 28 before a distinguished audience which included Cardinal John Henry Newman. The Birmingham choir and orchestra (in which Elgar played) gave Dvořák full support and although he had to use Deichmann, a German, leader of the second violins, as interpreter he had no difficulty in communicating his wishes. During that period Dvořák conducted eight concerts in four days. It was suggested to him that he might take Cardinal Newman's *Dream of Gerontius* as subject for an oratorio. He did not respond to this proposal, but he did agree to compose a *Requiem* for the Birmingham Festival of 1891. This is one of the outstanding settings of this text of the nineteenth century, less dramatic but more symphonic than Verdi's *Manzoni Requiem* (1874), and devotional without being overtly pious. Like all Dvořák's choral works the instrumentation is a vital factor, and notable use is made of the darker tones of cor anglais and bass clarinet. In 1886 he went to another of the great English Festivals, at Leeds, for which his cantata *St Ludmilla* (see p. 70) had been commissioned. During his rehearsals in Leeds Dvořák was helped by the Festival Director, Arthur Sullivan, who stood by to translate instructions for him. Dvořák spoke to Sullivan in German, which Sullivan understood because he had been educated in Leipzig. As in Birmingham Dvořák enjoyed an enormous success. At the end of the performance of *St Ludmilla*, according to *The Liverpool Mercury*:

... people stood up in the orchestra, in the gallery, and on the floor, and climbed on benches and chairs to cheer the composer. Girls in the chorus waved their handkerchiefs and joined their shrill treble to the general tumult. Men shouted and waved their hats, and such a Babel of rejoicing has rarely been witnessed anywhere ...

On October 28 Dvořák wrote his thanks to the Festival Secretary, and in his letter he said:

... The most beautiful voices of the ladies, and the powerful tenors and basses I never can forget! I was much moved and touched on hearing them. I would be very glad to kiss the hands of the ladies, and shake the hands of the gentlemen, but it is too late—I will leave it for another occasion.

St Ludmilla was given three performances in London after the Leeds premiere: "the enthusiasm—this English enthusiasm—" he wrote, "was such as I have not experienced for a long while." The enthusiasm remained. In 1890 Dvořák came to London to conduct the Symphony in G major (Op. 88) which, although performed a few weeks earlier in Prague, was the result of a commission from Novello. This symphony, a complete contrast to its predecessor, is a work of great lyrical beauty, a reflection of Dvořák's life at Vysoká, where he used to wander amid the hills and woods, to sit with the villagers in the village inn, to rear pigeons. In the middle of the third movement, the scherzo, Dvořák recollects a tune from his opera *The Stubborn Lovers*, the kind of spontaneous tune that reflects Dvořák's love of people, nature, and music.

8

mf

In 1891 Dvořák received an invitation from Charles
Villiers Stanford (1852–1924) to visit Cambridge, where it
was proposed to confer on him an honorary degree. The
invitation was duly accepted, but only a few days before
Dvořák was due to leave Prague Stanford was alarmed to
receive this postcard, dated May 26.

My dear friend:

I hear from the London newspaper of today that there is
much influenza in your country and on account of that I
and my wife are afraid to come there. The journey from
Prague to London is very long and if we had a bad
w^h_aether we can easy take cold—and what shall we do
there? Please tell us, what is to be done?

Ever yours,

Ant. Dvořák

Stanford was alarmed, because it was a rule at Cambridge
that an honorary degree could only be conferred in person.
He telegraphed back that the newspaper reports were
inaccurate, and on May 30 Dvořák sent another postcard
in which he said, ". . . I with pleasure see that no danger is
to the influenza . . ."

On June 15 he conducted a performance of his G major
Symphony and the *Stabat Mater* by the University Musical
Society, and next day he was made a Doctor of Music. He

*Dvořák in the robes of an Honorary Doctor of Music of
Cambridge University*

was thrilled by the splendour of the ceremony and amused that the proceedings were conducted in Latin. Others awarded honorary degrees at the same ceremony were Elie Metchnikov, the Russian scientist, the Bishop of Albany, U.S.A., and William Lecky, the Irish historian.

Five years later Dvořák came to England for the last time. Once again this was to launch a major work. The Violoncello Concerto in B minor (Op. 104) is one of the two or three finest works in this category. Written in New York and revised in Bohemia, it was played by Leo Stern at a concert of Dvořák's works at the Queen's Hall, on March 19, 1896. The programme also included the Symphony in D major and the *Biblical Songs* (with orchestral accompaniment).

7. Dvořák and Tchaikovsky

DVOŘÁK HAD LOOKED FORWARD to his first visit to England because, like many people in eastern Europe at that time, he believed that there the cause of national emancipation could be sympathetically understood. When he went to the United States he believed that liberty was a theme that would appeal to large numbers of idealists. The liberty of the Czechs was one side of Dvořák's simple political philosophy; another side was his support for pan-Slavism, the union of the interests of all the Slavonic peoples. This is indicated by the subjects of his operas—Polish and Russian as well as Czech—and by the general character of the folk-music basis of his works. In 1888, and again in 1890, he had opportunity to reaffirm this pan-Slavonic creed.

Tchaikovsky came to Prague in February, 1888, in order to conduct two concerts. Since he had a dislike of being openly involved in politics (involvement of this kind was not then always comfortable) he was somewhat alarmed to be met at Prague railway station by a large and demonstrative group, who were as anxious to welcome him as they were to show their distaste for their Austrian overlords. Privately, Tchaikovsky was delighted to discover how friendly the Czechs were towards the Russians. On February 14 and February 16 there were dinners in Tchaikovsky's honour, at which Dvořák was present. At the second of these dinners, given by the Russian Circle, Tchaikovsky made a short speech in Czech. He was pleased to have found time to visit Dvořák at home and wrote to his brother Modest how delighted he was with the Czechs—"great chaps", he said —and also to have made friends with Dvořák. Dvořák presented him with an autographed copy of the D minor Symphony.

Just at this time Dvořák was busy with his opera *The Jacobin*, which was produced in Prague on February 12, 1889. A story of intrigue, of virtue rewarded and wickedness punished, and set in Bohemia during Napoleonic times, *The Jacobin* was immediately successful. The picture of village life painted by Dvořák is irresistible. It is realistic, but generous, for Dvořák found it difficult (even in music) to dislike people. As always he uses many dance metres in the course of this work. At the very beginning we hear a waltz, the universal dance of the nineteenth century; in the ballet at the end of the opera there is a merry *polka* (Ex. 9, Ex. 10).

9

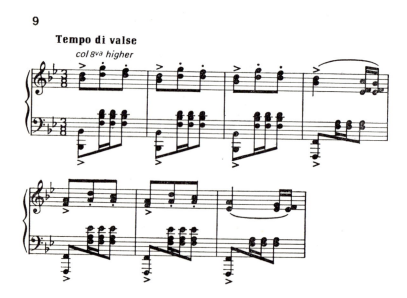

10

Dvořák had been greatly impressed by the "warm emotion" of Tchaikovsky's *Eugen Onegin* ("warm emotion" distinguishes Dvořák's own music) and had written to the composer to say so. Tchaikovsky wrote to thank Dvořák and a month later wrote another letter, on behalf of the Moscow Musical Society, to invite him to visit Russia.

Smetana had died in 1884, and it was natural that his place as the first Czech composer should come to be filled by Dvořák, whose reputation by now stood so high in other countries as well as his own. In 1889 he was asked to become a teacher in the Prague Conservatory. This at that time he was disinclined to do, since he had so many other things to occupy his mind. But in 1891 he agreed to undertake the post of composition professor. Among his pupils were Josef Suk (1874–1935), who married Dvořák's daughter in 1898, Oskar Nebdal (1874–1930), Vitěszlav Novák (1870–1949), and Rudolf Karel (1880–1945), all of whom were to play important roles in the music of Czechoslovakia.

At this time Dvořák was honoured by the Emperor Franz Joseph, who awarded him the Order of the Iron Cross; by the Charles University, which made him an honorary Doctor of Philosophy; and by the Academy of Sciences and Art in Prague, and the Academy of Sciences in Berlin, both of which elected him a member. In October, 1889, Dvořák conducted a concert in Dresden and was present in Berlin and Hamburg when Hans von Bülow (1830–94) introduced the D minor Symphony to German audiences.

In March, 1890, Dvořák visited Russia, conducting performances of his works both in Moscow and Petrograd. The Symphony in D minor made a profound impression, and so did the *Stabat Mater*, which was performed by the German Choir in Moscow. Anton Rubinstein (1829–94), Leopold Auer (1845–1930), and Herman Laroche (1845–1904), were among those at a complimentary dinner who heaped praises on Dvořák. Laroche, indeed, advised Russian composers to study Dvořák's music and to take a hint from this representative of a small, neighbouring country. Dvořák had good reason to be pleased.

During this climactic period Dvořák had put some of his philosophical ideas into three overtures: "In Nature's Realm" (Op. 91), "Carnival" (Op. 92), and "Othello" (Op. 93). These three works (of which the middle one alone is at all well-known) were thought of as a unified whole, to be included within the general title *Nature, Life and Love*. The first of the three overtures is a painting of a summer evening—with the light breeze in the rustle of tremolo strings, the stolid repeated bass notes of a rustic band, the unmistakable sound of birds, the kind of "hymn to nature", that are typical of such "naturalistic" music. Dvořák's "programme" music, however, is not so limited in reference that it may not be enjoyed for its own sake.

"In Nature's Realm" is an essay in praise of happy solitude—of solitude that, in fact, is no solitude. "Carnival" carries the "Nature" motiv of the first overture into the crowded life of festival time. This whirligig of sound is the idealisation of the fairs of long ago in Nelahozeves; but also of fairs all over the world. It is vulgar, as is Tchaikovsky's *Italian Capriccio;* but so is life. "Carnival" opens in this way:

11a

After a view of many aspects of life at carnival time the end of the day brings this riot of chord colour:

11b

"Carnival" is one of the most frequently performed of Dvořák's works. The third of this set of symphonic overtures, "Othello", is heard much less frequently. It is, however, a beautiful and serious work, pointing the moral that life can be beautiful, and love perfect, where jealousy does not prevail.

The three overtures, conducted by the composer, were given at a Farewell Concert in Prague, on April 28, 1892.

8. Dvořák and the
United States

MRS JEANETTE THURBER, of New York, had a great deal
both of money and of idealism. She invested some of both in
an operatic venture in New York, and when this failed the
rest went into a National Conservatory of Music. This was
founded in 1885 as a non-profit-making institution which,
where necessary, would provide free tuition. Mrs Thurber
wished to develop a thoroughly representative American
school of composition, and for this reason no prospective
students were excluded on account of race or creed. The
first Director of the National Conservatory was Jacques
Bouhy (1848–1929), a Belgian singer and singing-teacher.
Bouhy returned to Europe in 1889.

On the advice of a Viennese friend, Mrs Thurber ap-
proached Dvořák with a tentative contract. He, however,
was not eager to leave Bohemia, his friends, and his obligations there, and gave her little encouragement. But Mrs
Thurber was persistent, and in the end Dvořák, having
taken advice from friends and having arranged to be absent
from his teaching commitments in Prague, accepted the
appointment on a two-year basis. Shortly before he left
Prague for the United States, he had a commission from Mrs
Thurber to write a work in honour of the four-hundredth
anniversary of Columbus's arrival in America. The work
was to be a cantata setting of *The American Flag*, one of
Joseph Rodman Drake's (1795–1820) posthumously pub-

lished poems. Since Dvořák had no possibility of fulfilling Mrs Thurber's commission at that time he substituted a convenient, all-purpose, *Te Deum*.

Dvořák took his wife and two of their children to New York as well as Josef Kovařík, who accompanied him as secretary and assistant. He took a lower Midtown apartment (327, East 17 Street) which was his base all the time he was in the U.S.A. In New York Dvořák avoided social life as much as possible. He preferred walking in Central Park, or going to see the railway locomotives at Grand Central and Pennsylvania stations, or the ocean liners on the Hudson River, to smart parties. Since he was expected to found a school of composition, he set about it in the only way he knew how. He found what music there was that could be considered as native American folk-music for his students to study, absorb, and use as he himself had used European folk-music. He recommended making a start with Indian and negro melodies —Dvořák was drawn to a study of Indian culture through reading the story of *Hiawatha* in Czech translation, and he collected as many examples of Indian melodies as he could. With the negroes he felt an instinctive sympathy, and in an interview with the *New York Herald* he said this:

> In the negro melodies of America I find all that is needed for a great and noble school of music. They are pathetic, tender, passionate, melancholy, bold, merry, gay, or what you will. There is nothing in the whole range of composition which cannot be supplied from this source. . . . I am satisfied that the future music of this country must be founded on what are called the negro melodies.

Mrs Jeanette Thurber

It is likely that he came across William Francis Allen's edition of *Slave Songs of the United States* (published 1867). The melodies of this collection inspired Henry F. Gilbert (1868–1928), whose *Negro Episode* was the second of his *Two Episodes* (Op. 2, no. 2) for orchestra of 1897.

Dvořák did not mean quite what he said, or, perhaps, did not say quite what he meant. Being concerned for people he was interested in all kinds of music that had special social significance. As a musician he was alive to the inspirational qualities to be found in any unfamiliar idiom. In the winter of 1892–3 he sketched a symphony, which was completed in May, 1893. This symphony contained ideas at least to be found both in negro and Indian music. The style, however, was Dvořák's own, so that the Symphony in E minor "From the New World" (Op. 95) is a series of observations on the American scene by a Bohemian composer. The second movement, famous because of its moving cor anglais melody, was said to have been inspired by Dvořák's reading of the scene "Funeral in the Forest" in Longfellow's *Song of Hiawatha*. This famous poem had been published in a new edition, with Frederick Remington's drawings, in 1890.

Of Dvořák's American pupils, the most important were Harvey Worthington Loomis (1865–1930), Henry Thacker Burleigh (1866–1949), and Rubin Goldmark (1872–1936). Loomis was an authority on Indian folk-music, on which he organised his own personal style. Burleigh's singing of negro spirituals first made Dvořák aware of this rich tradition, and by his arrangements Burleigh made them widely popular in the United States. Goldmark, who used negro music in such works as his *Negro Rhapsody*, became Director of the Juilliard Graduate School, in New York, where he taught both George Gershwin and Aaron Copland, two composers whose descent from Dvořák is, perhaps, not all that difficult to discover from their music.

Josef Kovařík's father had emigrated to the U.S.A. He was organist at Spillville, Iowa. In the summer of 1893, the Dvořáks went with Kovařík to stay at Spillville. Dvořák related how those of his compatriots who lived here had mostly come some forty years previously. Then, he said, they were "all the poorest of the poor"; now, "after great hardship and struggle they are very well off here". The

Czech colony at Spillville were delighted to welcome their guests, with news of far-distant Bohemia. Dvořák loved Spillville and wandered about the countryside listening to the song of the birds, which he put into the Scherzo of his String Quartet in F major. In this extract the birds seem to sing in all four parts.

12

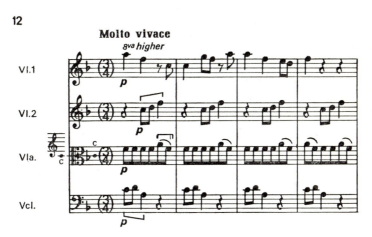

In Spillville Dvořák encountered a group of Iroquois Indians, whose music is supposed to have suggested the percussive rhythms of the first movement and the scherzo of the String Quintet in E flat (Op. 97). This work was also composed in Spillville.

In August the Dvořáks went to Chicago for a Czech Festival which was held there during The World Fair, and they went to visit another Czech community, at Omaha, Nebraska.

On December 16, 1893, the Symphony in E minor, conducted by Anton Seidl (1830–98), a Hungarian conductor who had once been Wagner's assistant in Bayreuth, was given its first performance at a New York Philharmonic Society concert in Carnegie Hall. It was greeted rapturously,

E

and the composer was awarded a special prize by the National Conservatory.

Dvořák said of this work, "I should never have written the symphony like I have, if I hadn't seen America." What precisely he meant by this is not certain. Although there is a possible influence of negro and Indian melodic idiom this is neither so strong nor so obvious as to obtrude. Rather, perhaps, one should detect an attempt to address an audience directly—without the complexities of German argument that are often seen to belong to the tradition of the post-classical symphony. The "New World" Symphony is tuneful; it is less remarkable for the strength of its musical logic. The first and last movements particularly are confined by the caption-like quality of the principal motivs, which are seen to appear rather more often than the music really requires.

In the spring of 1894 the Dvořáks went home, where the composer was fêted both in Prague and in Vysoká. In Klin where he lived, Tchaikovsky, having become rich, endowed a village school. In Vysoká Dvořák, who was richer than he could ever have thought possible, gave a new church organ to the village. On July 20, 1894, the "New World" Symphony was given its European premiere at Carlsbad (Karlovy Vary), the spa town on the Czech-German border. On October 13 Dvořák conducted its first performance in Prague, in a concert of his own works, and three days later set off once again for the U.S.A.

His second visit was brief, for this time he was even less inclined to leave his own country, and he knew that his influence was needed at home rather than abroad. There was not really much more that he could do towards creating a "national school of composition" in the U.S.A. He had al-

Carnegie Hall

ready done much, but inspirationally rather than administratively. His second visit lasted six months, during which time he was made an honorary member of the New York Philharmonic Society. He also composed the Cello Concerto at this time, and began a String Quartet in A flat (Op. 105). In 1893 Dvořák completed *The American Flag*, which he had been asked to compose before he went to the U.S.A. It was not performed until after he had left the country for good. To many Americans of that time this plain-spoken "Apostrophe to the Eagle" seemed the right point of departure for a "national music".

13

9. *The Death of Brahms*

DURING THE LAST DECADE of the nineteenth century the evidence of success in the struggle to establish a Czech national identity was to be seen in various aspects of life in Prague. In 1890 the Czech Academy of Sciences and Arts was founded. Not only was Dvořák a member of this institution, but he was a friend of the architect J. Hlávka, President of the Academy, on whose initiative it had been founded. After his return from the United States, and his last visit to London, Dvořák was a frequent visitor to the Academy, where his music was often played. In 1891 the spread of interest in literature in Prague was marked by the opening of a new Musical Library. In 1892 four students of the Prague Conservatory of Music (K. Hoffmann, J. Suk, O. Nedbal, and O. Berger) formed a String Quartet. Recommended by Hanuš Wihan to the Chamber Music Society, they gave their inaugural recital on October 22. It was a brilliant success and soon afterwards, this ensemble, now called the Bohemian String Quartet, performed with notable success in Vienna and Berlin.

In 1894 the members of the National Theatre Orchestra —which for many years had been the principal concert-giving orchestra in Prague—formed a Philharmonic Society with the purpose of regularising the annual series of Symphony Concerts. On January 4, 1896, the Czech Philharmonic Orchestra, soon to become one of the leading orchestras in Europe, gave its first concert. The performance consisted of works by Dvořák, who conducted the concert.

It was an era of optimism, reflected in the broadest way in an All-Slav Exhibition that took place in Prague in 1895. Industrialisation had brought benefits to the Czechs, and much prosperity to the middle class. Nationalism which once had existed only underground was now almost respectable. Dvořák, who had never made any secret of his loyalties, reacted to the hope in the air by zealously carrying out what he conceived as his national duty. He was regular in his commitments at the Conservatory of Music, and strenuous in his support of young artists of all kinds. He saw much of the writer Jaroslav Vrchlický (1853–1912), from whom he had had the text for *St Ludmilla*, and once again read the works of Karel Erben (1811–70), who had provided him with the story of *The Spectre's Bride*.

On February 16, 1896 Dvořák was in Vienna for a performance of the "New World" Symphony, conducted by Richter. Brahms was present too, and the two composers sat together in the directors' box. Not long afterwards further attempts were made to try to persuade Dvořák to settle permanently in Vienna, where he was to be offered a professorship of composition in the Conservatory. Brahms was so anxious that Dvořák should settle in the Austrian capital that when Dvořák said that it would cost too much to make the change he offered himself to make up any financial loss. He was enchanted with the Cello Concerto that had its premiere in London on March 19. After playing through the work with Robert Hausmann, the cellist of the Joachim Quartet, he said, "Had I known that such a cello concerto as that could be written I would have tried to compose one myself."

After composing the "New World" Symphony and the Cello Concerto Dvořák wrote the String Quartet in G major

The National Theatre, Prague

71

(Op. 106), in which he summarised his attitudes to classical music. The formal structures are important, but not more than their functional role allows. For this is music eloquent with feeling, and the feeling is unmistakable. Dvořák here allows the sorrows and strains of life, hinted at in the slow movement, to be resolved in the genial atmosphere of the Bohemian countryside. These contrasts are shown below in the solemn opening of the slow movement, and in the middle section of the scherzo, than which nothing could be simpler! But it will be seen that there are resemblances in these excerpts. Compare the 5th bar of the first with the 1st of the second.

14a

14b

It is not easy today to appreciate how, at that time, there could have been so much angry debate as to whether music should be "about" nothing or something. The promoters of "classical" music (among whom Brahms was accepted as the leader) not only believed that music should be abstract and not to be explained by, or to explain, other media, but that music which had any other aim was in some way unwholesome. That is to say, of course, music in the concert-hall. Opera, perhaps, was a different matter. Dvořák was not given to splitting hairs with theorists or dogmatists. He was a practical musician. Yet he had his ideals. These entered into his desire to justify the simple kind of people from whom he came, and to serve the national cause. As we have seen, after his return from the United States the national situation was more encouraging than it had been before. In 1896, then, he settled down to the composition of three symphonic poems which should express this fact.

Karel Erben (see p. 70) was most loved by Czechs for his *The Garland* (*Kytice*), a collection of poems based on folk-legends, and the verse technique of the old ballads. Erben spent thirty years of his life working in the field of folk-lore and folk-art. Dvořák took four of Erben's poems from *The Garland* and wrote musical commentaries on them in the form of symphonic poems. These were *The Water Goblin*, *The Noonday Witch*, and *The Golden Spinning Wheel*. The ballads as told by Erben were allegorical; the forces of evil being represented by creatures of the supernatural world able to intervene at will in human affairs. The stories came out of a far past, from people who lived in the mountains and often in fear. In the nineteenth century such stories, as noticed on p. 74, had a symbolic value. Somehow they were or could be related to the life of the nation. Bohemia, like the victims of the legends, could seem to be taken below the dark waters by the evil "goblin", or seized by the "noonday witch", or betrayed by a "step-mother".

Dvořák grasped the picturesque quality of the ballads, and

these symphonic poems show some of his most beautiful "programme" music. Whether he recognised their deeper significance is more doubtful, for psychological analysis was not yet fashionable. Besides, being inclined to think the best of people he was not at his happiest when trying to depict evil in terms of music. In any case, in Dvořák's optimistic creed good in the end should prevail over evil.

The three symphonic poems were performed in Prague on June 6, 1896. They were subsequently performed in Vienna and, in 1897, in the city of Brno. On April 11 *The Water Goblin* was presented at a Brno Philharmonic Society Concert, conducted by Janáček; the other two works were given under the same auspices a month later, this time with Dvořák conducting. Each of these works made a deep impression, — an impression to quote his own word, of "truthfulness" — on Janáček, who at that time was greatly occupied in the study of folk-lore and folk-music.

A few months after the completion of the three symphonic poems mentioned above Dvořák began the composition of another, *The Wild Dove*, also based on a ballad by Erben. This is the most telling of the pieces inspired by Erben. It is also the most realistic. The story tells how a girl-widow follows the coffin of her dead husband to the funeral, and how she seems inconsolable. But it was she who killed her husband. She marries again, but afterwards, stricken with a great sense of her guilt, she kills herself. The wild dove, as it were, comments on the action, and in the end it is the voice of the dove that maddens the guilty woman. Whatever else the work is, or is not, it is a wonderful picture of village life as it was — of life as it is.

Early in 1897 Dvořák received further honours in Vienna. Together with Grieg — in whose career Brahms was also greatly interested—he was made an honorary member of the Society of Friends of Music. He was also made a member of the Austrian State Committee, by which he had been helped at the outset of his career. He took the place of Brahms on this Committee, whose death in April, 1897, caused Dvořák, who was always conscious of the debt he owed to him, great sorrow. For some months after the death of his friend Dvořák composed nothing.

Scene from a performance of Rusalka *at the National Theatre*

10. *"Most suitable for the Nation"*

WHEN HE THOUGHT ABOUT COMPOSING AGAIN, Dvořák contemplated his output so far as it had gone, and his role as the principal mouthpiece of the Bohemian people. Since his works were played all over the world, reaching where words could not reach, he saw that he had a special responsibility.

Brahms had been the great exponent of abstract music, but at the time of his death Dvořák had moved away from Brahms's principles. His four symphonic poems of 1896 were quite contrary to Brahms's ideas, both in practice and in ideal. In 1897 Dvořák added one more symphonic poem to his list. This, *The Hero's Song*, however, was not based on any literary theme; it is intended, so the composer said, to illustrate his own career. This work was first performed in Vienna on December 4, 1898, with Gustav Mahler conducting. At the end of January, 1899, it was introduced to the Czechs at a Philharmonic Concert in Prague.

Dvořák, of course, had no need to compose such a work. The story of his own life is illustrated in his works as a whole, and it required no separate "programme" piece. But Dvořák felt he had to write this last symphonic poem, just as many people feel an urge to write their literary autobiography. He did, however, feel that he had more important things to do; for he had seen a new opera libretto by Adolf Wenig.

The story of *The Devil and Kate* is one of the best ever offered to Dvořák—both romantic and realistic. It is the story of a village scold who, unable to find a partner with

76

whom to dance, says that she would dance with the devil himself—were he to turn up at the county fair. In fact he does turn up, but finally discovers how much better it would have been for him if he had never encountered Kate. *The Devil and Kate* is also a study of how badly landlords once treated their tenants. Dvořák in this opera combines comedy with homily. The lady of the manor, who exploited her tenants, was in danger of going down to hell—a prospect not at all pleasing to her. Since she repented she was spared this discomfort, and the opera ends happily.

The Devil and Kate is bound together in Wagnerian manner by motivs representing the main groups of characters in the opera—the villagers, their overlords, and the devils. There are also many dances in the opera, and these again are carefully allotted so as to give more definition to character.

After *The Devil and Kate* Dvořák wrote *Rusalka*, a fairy-tale opera, to a libretto by Jaroslav Kvapil. This is the story of a prince who falls in love with a water-nymph, but, under a curse, dies when Rusalka, the water-nymph, has to return to the water whence she came. *Rusalka*, full of beautiful music describing nature, was very much loved by the Czechs, and it remains one of Dvořák's most popular works. The last of his operas was *Armida*, a story from the time of the medieval crusades in the Holy Land which had been made into an opera by other, earlier, composers. The libretto for Dvořák's opera was written by Vrchlický, the greatest literary figure among the Czechs at the beginning of this century. The opera was produced on March 25, 1904, but was a failure. Dvořák was hurt. He had laboured to produce something for "the people", and it was rejected.

The reason for Dvořák's devotion to opera was founded on an ideal. On March 1, 1904, he gave an interview to a

Vienna newspaper, in which he said that "opera [was] the most suitable [kind of music] for the nation. This music is listened to by the broad masses—whereas when I compose a symphony I might have to wait years for it to be performed."

Two months later Dvořák was dead. He had enjoyed good health all his life, but now in the early months of 1904 he was very far from well. In April he was not well enough to attend the Musical Festival—the first of the famous "Spring Festivals"—in Prague which began with his *Ludmilla*.

On May 1 Dvořák suffered a cerebral haemorrhage, and four days later the streets of Prague were filled with a sad and silent crowd, wishing to bid farewell to one of the greatest and most loved Czechs. Dvořák's body lay in state in the Church of St Salvator, and was buried in the Vysehrad Cemetary where great Czechs were traditionally buried.

What Dvořák meant to his people was understood a long time ago—a surprisingly long time ago. In introducing him to the people of Leeds in 1886 a writer in the Festival Programme for that year stated:

. . . Had he been merely a musician, with no thought or feeling outside his art, he would probably have drifted away into some small German town and been absorbed into the huge mob of Teutonic musicianship. But, sprung from the Bohemian people, brought up amongst them, and remaining of them heart and soul, he acted the part of a good Czech, stayed at home and joined in the struggle of Slav against German culture [and Austrian rule] . . . Dvořák is a great Czech. This fact explains much that would otherwise be obscure.

Of another composer Dvořák once said: "Mozart is sunshine". That may also be applied to Dvořák himself, in more than one sense, and may best serve as his epitaph.

Index

References to illustrations are shown in italic type

79

Printed in Great Britain by The Bowering Press, Plymouth